CR(

Poetry by Asian, Afric

KISS

Kiss
Poetry by Asian, African, Caribbean and Chinese writers

First published in 1994 by Crocus

Crocus books are published by
Commonword Ltd
Cheetwood House,
21 Newton Street,
Manchester M1 1FZ.

(c) Commonword Ltd and the authors.

No part of this publication may be reproduced without written permission, except in the case of brief extracts embodied in critical articles, reviews or lectures. For information contact Commonword Ltd.

Commonword gratefully acknowledges financial assistance from the Association of Greater Manchester Authorities, North West Arts Board and Manchester City Council.

Crocus Books are distributed by Password (Books) Ltd, 23 New Mount Street, Manchester M4 4DE.

Cover image by Alan Jones. Cover design by Hemisphere, 47 Newton Street, Manchester M1 1FT.
Produced by Caxton's Final Film, 16 Nicholas Street, Manchester M1 4EJ.
Printed by Shanleys, 16 Belvoir St., Tonge Fold, Bolton.

British Library Cataloguing-in-Publication Data. A catalogue record for this book is available from the British Library.

Contents

Introduction   ix

Love Poem *Lemn Sissay*   1
Perfume *John Siddique*   2
A Love Story *Seni Seneviratne*   3
Ngoh Hei Foon Nei *Tang Lin*   4
Self And Selfish *Shamsa Butt*   6
The Lovers (Deewane) *Komal Purwaha*   7
Embers *Deyika Nzeribe*   8
Mithai *Maya Chowdhry*   9
The Chef's Song *Pete Kalu*   10
A Time In The South Pacific No.7 *John Siddique*   11
Dreaming Of You *Zareen Zahid Hussain*   12
Blue-beat Heart *Muhammad Khalil Eugene Lange*   13
The Colour Black *Quibilah Montsho*   14
In Darkness *Zareen Zahid Hussain*   16
Love Poetry *SuAndi*   17
Reflection *Tang Lin*   18
Love Is...Unfathomable *Tina Tamsho*   19
'Rika, can you hear me?' *Milan Ghosh*   21
Lost In The Post *Cheryl Martin*   22
Prove It *Quibilah Montsho*   24
You In Me *Kosar Saira*   26
Shall I Compare Thee? *Debjani Chatterjee*   27
Never Have A Poem Called Love *Quibilah Montsho*   28
Melanin *Levi Tafari*   29
Hour-glass *Saqib Deshmukh*   30
The Calling *Lemn Sissay*   31

Seeds Of Ras Tafari *John Lyons*	32
Love Poem *Saqib Deshmukh*	34
September's Song *Jaya Graves*	35
Never *Kosar Saira*	36
The Crying Rain (Barsaat) *Komal Purwaha*	37
Saturday Night *Saqib Deshmukh*	39
Your Face, My Heart *Quibilah Montsho*	40
Untitled *John Chombi*	41
To My Mother *Tang Lin*	42
Something In The Air *Seni Seneviratne*	44
8 am *Milan Ghosh*	45
Snatched Moments *Frances Rahman*	46
Sincerity And Innocence *Tang Lin*	47
Throw Your Love Away *Męi-Chi Chan*	49
Love And Lust *Milan Ghosh*	50
Eastern Senses *Selina Deen*	51
Next Time *Seni Seneviratne*	52
T. *Zareen Zahid Hussain*	53
You Can't Catch It By Kissing *Tina Tamsho*	54
The Kissing Ritual *John Siddique*	55
Hands *SuAndi*	56
Celtic Knots *Maya Chowdhry*	57
The Poet's Song *Pete Kalu*	59
Heart, Don't Break (Dil Na Toote) *Komal Purwaha*	60
Kissing Asians *Saqib Deshmukh*	61
For Love's Sake *SuAndi*	62
The Edge *Maya Chowdhry*	63
Cherries Maya Chowdhry	64
That - You And Me *Kosar Saira*	65
The Sweet Smell Of Success *Lorraine Scott*	67
Sunset *Samir Chatterjee*	68
Smile *Na Oyo Quartey*	70

A Cup Of You *Scorcha*	71
Love's Blow *John Chombi*	73
Look At The Weather *Timothy Wesley*	74
Have You Ever Felt The Breeze *Lorraine Scott*	75
Veneer *Rodney Taylor*	76
I Never Can Say Goodbye *Quibilah Montsho*	77
Forbidden Love *Aaron Rouse*	78
Emotion *Victoria McKenzie*	79
Final Demand *Elaine Okoro*	80
Lust + Love = Forever *Gloria Knowles*	82
Roaring Lion *Paulette Browne*	83
Love *Trudy Blake*	84
To Love You *Prince Marley*	86
Integration *Frances Rahman*	87
Found *Shamsa Butt*	88
The Fat Man's Song *Pete Kalu*	89
When Spirit Moved *Tang Lin*	90
Perfume (Kushboo) *Saqib Deshmukh*	92
Shadows *Jaya Graves*	93
Quibilah *Kosar Saira*	94
Avenue *Maya Chowdhry*	95
Purple Heart *Seni Seneviratne*	97
Marriage *SuAndi*	99
If You Leave *SuAndi*	100
Again *Deyika Nzeribe*	101
Culture And Assimilation *Shamsa Butt*	102
Labouring Lost Love *Sua Huab*	103
Change Not Blame *Sua Huab*	104
In A New Land *Mei-Chi Chan*	105
Splitting Up *Mei-Chi Chan*	106
Biographies	107

Introduction

Love is an international language. It is instantly understood around the world. And like all living languages it is constantly on the move, changing as society itself changes. For each generation of lovers, love means something different.

This collection of eighty eight poems is the work of forty contemporary black writers coming from a great diversity of cultural backgrounds, life experiences, schools and vocations. Their achievement has been to fashion with words the cut and shape of love for black people in the UK today. Occupations of the contributors range from PhD student to commis chef. A few are novices when it comes to writing. Many have won major awards. This collection will surprise. It contains poems which are unashamedly modern in either style or content, or both. Topics tackled include safe sex, the madness and ecstasy of falling in love, and the agony of splitting up. Love and urban life, the love of the self and of one's own culture, cross-cultural marriages, adultery, chastity, passion and intimacy are all explored.

This is not a book hatched by academics. It has a raw, energising vibrance and abundance and displays a wealth of approaches to the subject. There are poems which are rhapsodic, others moody, others revolutionary, still others coolly detached and philosophical. For some of the contributors love is a celebration, others advocate caution, one or two advise you to abandon all hope if you fall in love, but do so anyway!

The sources of inspiration are many. South Asian, Rastafarian, Celtic and Chinese influences are detectable. There are dub rhythms, runes, haiku, raps, lyrical and melodic styles at play. The settings range from bedsits to cars to doorways to hotel lobbies to cafes to waterbeds, and the relationships from heterosexual to lesbian and gay.

Kiss projects black love in all its forms, shades and colours. That we as black people, in the face of all external prejudice, bigotry and injustice, and the general hassles and vicissitudes of life, find the strength to keep loving at all, is a feat in itself. As the international dub poet, Martin Glynn puts it, the book is '*a testimony to the fact that our humanity, despite efforts to distort and destroy it, will always take priority over those things which affect our lives in an adverse sense.*'

Sincere thanks to Tang Lin and Quibilah Montsho for their work on the editing panel.

Pete Kalu
Cultureword worker.

Love Poem

Lemn Sissay

You remind me
define me
incline me

If you died
I'd

Perfume

John Siddique

O with the smell of oil and flowers.

With Samarkand and Sandalwood anoint me.

Bathe deep in rose-water

and walk as shimmering light
dappled on the ground
        everywhere.

There must be incense.
this serpent loves the smell.

Plait flowers for me.

With Betel leaf reddening your lips
kiss me
    kiss me.

A Love Story

Seni Seneviratne

She fell in love
           with a layout artist
Who had passionate designs
                   on her
Together they pasted up
            a plan
Typeset promises
         neatly laid out
But then
         it all came unstuck
She didn't know
              what to blame
Except
    the
            poor
          quality
                    of
              the
                    cow-gum

Ngoh Hei Foon Nei

Tang Lin

moon light
silver
I like you

thunder lightning
strike
emotion to describe loving
I like you

your sweet
dripping tongue
tasting kiss
I like you   I like you   I like you

I like you
in a thousand million voices
I will whisper
into your ear

ngoh hei foon nei

lies divide
your heart and my heart

lies camouflage
vision and sound

lies

ping ding dong
zee zer zeee
like human emotions

respect   acceptance   welcoming   loving
    caring   warmth

like
I like you

ngoh hei foon nei

Self And Selfish

Shamsa Butt

The purest love
Is totally unselfish
Love.
But nothing
Is more selfish
Than love.

The Lovers

Komal Purwaha

Let me be swept away in the sea
  of tears,
Let me sleep on a bed of thorns,
Leave me alone, let me be,
My heart is crazy for him...

Deewane

Ashkon ke nadi mein beheh jaane
  do,
Kaanton par mujhe soane do,
Duniyawale mujhe mere haal pe
  choor do,
Mera dil unka deewana hai...

Embers

Deyika Nzeribe

So we sat
Ember-like in
That cafe,
Sipping our coffees.
'...I mean,' she said,
Ending,
'All we'll ever
Have in common is
The past.'
I took another sip.
Lump in my throat,
I didn't know what
To say.
I didn't know what
She meant.

Sounded good though.

Mithai

Maya Chowdhry

Your flowers lasted
through a full moon
and past,
the white blooms
whispered sometimes
while I slept.

I sweetened the water
from which
they drank,
and hoped my
kisses were not too sweet.

I sung while the lips
of lilies opened buds
the sticky flesh
closing my
fingers picked.

I sent you burfi and ladoo
in a box and ribbon,
and know they were
too sweet
but hoped my
kisses lasted longer
than the taste of Indian sweets.

The Chef's Song

Pete Kalu

Food is the
food of love
and I want
to swallow you
whole

A Time In The South Pacific No. 7

John Siddique

One time in the South Pacific
we sat as rocks
immobile
with heads like flowers made of tiny shells.

I am bound to you by raffia-like emotion.
I am bound into the parcel of myself.

Bound tobacco leaves
guarded by fierce pearls.

Kept in 2 bundles.
This wish, to be a cigarette with you,
burning for five minutes.
Then the closed doors won't matter
anymore.

Our nicotine will yellowly line the
ceiling and walls.
   and no one will know.

Dreaming Of You

Zareen Zahid Hussain

soothing
silences
in misty twilight,
lying, listening
to my
fevered heartbeats,
tasting
the
sweet urgency
of
their need,
gently gliding,
to a
welcoming,
watery
sleep.

Blue-beat Heart

Muhammad Khalil Eugene Lange

I paas tru yuhr nayburhood,
and I woz lookin out feh yuh.
Felt dhis song staat comin tru,
and knew jus wha' meh 'ad fe duh.
Walkin aan dhe street yuh live,
Meh 'ave so much luv fe give.
Meh travel deep inna I past,
to where dhe dice of luv were cast,

And dhen dhe music starts,
playin wid dhe strings of I heart.
And dhen dhe music starts,
playin with dhe strings of I heart.

I paasd by dhe old estate,
inna meh mind I meditate,
Memories of yuh relate to
melodies in blue.
In amonkst dhe ruins
dher's a melancholy tune,
dhat tells an old-old story,
nothink very new.

Aantill dhe music starts
playing wid dhe strings of I heart.
And dhen dhe music starts,
playin with dhe strings of I heart.

The Colour Black

Quibilah Montsho

Black smoke
Lays dust on
The charcoal board;
The black swan
Hides in the moon's eclipse.
My black Jaguar
Confuses the
Tarmac's haze,
And sheds big black books
In the night.

The black woman stands
With the eclipse on her back,
And meets with her black lover.
Black palms join
Like halves of one aubergine
Made-to-measure
Ebony style.

Black skin
Wraps around black skin
Lick wet fingers
Arms and legs
One black body
Smooth velvet
Rubs across satin sheen
Each knowing

The other's coolness.

Together
They turn
To face the round black
Of the concealed moon.
Looking into the darkness
The walk homewards
Seems breathtaking.

In Darkness

Zareen Zahid Hussain

waiting
in
rising desolation.
listening
for the birth
of
fantasised
footsteps,
breathing
the
vacuum
of used
human
dreams.
hopes
and illusions
slowly
seeping
away.

Love Poetry

SuAndi

Should I write of love. -
    Me. -
        Not I -
A political non voter
Rising on the tide of sexism, -
    Racism.
Love is wasted in these times of ours.
Energy sapping.
Mapping out days in kisses.
Embracing when there is an urgent call -
    To arm/s. -
        All our defences.
Lest the enemy reveals himself.
Dressed civilian -
    Appearing normal.
Hungry like a child orphaned.
Needing love.
Should I write of he,
And speak clearly of myself kissed -
    Into wakening.
That yesterday passed in a flurry of words -
    Now silent.
Now I am vibrant!
Should I write of love. -
    Me.
And waste energy,
When words cannot describe
Fire.

Reflection

Tang Lin

sun rises
moon shines
river hushes
you kiss me
you touch me
you make love to me

Love Is...Unfathomable

Tina Tamsho

I love you
but sometimes
love is a reason
for leaving.

Doors have closed
between us.
Wide chasms opened,
Divided us.

The universe is mighty
love
insignificant,
change
inevitable.

Still,
I love you.

The universe is mighty
We are insignificant,
but I have seen The Milky Way
with you by my side.

Together
we looked beyond our world,

Together
we were trapped,
not quite knowing
how to leave it all...
behind.

'Rika, can you hear me?'

Milan Ghosh

Rika, can you hear me?
For my soul is about to leave you
Yet it grieves for you, like trees
                        for the summer sun.
For everything is cold now, and bitter
With the mourning of Summer's end
Until the Spring of awakening life
When everything grows
How? Nobody knows, for like the wind
It comes and goes.
But we do not see it
Nor can we be it
And my hopes like the dove, are only
the things of love, which fly gracefully
for a moment in time that is all too
short, then land gently as leaves
from trees on a still Autumn day,
which decay and rot

in the cool valley of the past
                      that will never come back.

Lost In The Post

Cheryl Martin

My ex now talks
exclusively
to household appliances.
He's especially fond
of his ironing board.
They get along well,
since he's so anal-
retentive-compulsively-neat
that he still wears creases
in his jeans.
He likes clean things,
wipes the telephone white
after every day's non-use.

He writes me, sometimes.
I got a letter today that he started in July,
finished first week of October,
mailed in Nearly-November.
Told me, helpfully,
that he can't actually talk to me
in person
because knowing that I had loved him
makes him claustrophobic.
In a letter, we are one.
Face to face, he's asexual.
Silent. Would rather have a natter

with his coffee machine.
But on paper--
hell, I married somebody else, anyway.

And I've got a note
from four years ago
in which he states
categorically
that without love there is nothing.
Let's see the hoover top that.

Prove It

Quibilah Montsho

Evidence
My black hair
Curled into
Two
Of your
Silver
Earrings.

Proof
That
I have
Been
Close to you
Hugged you
Kissed your face
And your hair.

Evidence
Of
My
Attachment to you.

Evidently
I have
Loved you
Bodily
Sexually

My hair
Twisted
Around
Your jewels
As my black body
Wraps itself
Around yours.

Curious
How
Two hairs
Tell
So many
Stories of love.

You In Me

Kosar Saira

I love
Your voice
The way you speak
You're so intelligent
The way you think
Your logic

Your company
I never want to end
What's the matter with me
I miss you when we're apart
I am frightened
Of this endless obsession

You've taken over my whole life
My every heartbeat
Every thought
My every movement
You are the only need I have

You seem to be
In All of me

Shall I Compare Thee?

Debjani Chatterjee

The quills of busy ancestors
spluttered ecstatic over women
who swayed, graceful like Indian elephants
seen from behind as they strolled.
Majestic rolled their love.

But when I regard you, love of my life,
bull elephants do not come to mind,
nor even one-horned white rhinos -
though you are certainly rare.

The balm of your smile is a generous lake
I learn to swim in and discover
erupting volcanoes below the calm -
your nature is fashioned on the grand scale
but nothing comes close to your measure.

You are your own silent sweetness,
my dream mid summer night's richness.
It is joy when I touch you, glory to kiss you,
into throbbing, loving tenderness.

Never Have A Poem Called Love

Quibilah Montsho

Love looks like two people, lost in each other's eyes,
Unaware of the environment
Never shifting their gaze.
It is holding someone in your arms for hours,
Never loosening that support
Never growing tired.

Love sounds like heavy breathing
Each breath becoming deeper
Hearts beating faster and harder.

It is breakfast, lunch and dinner
My armchair and double bed

Love feels like two hands joined, palm to palm
Fingertips touching fingertips.

It lives in the pouring rain when it drenches us.

Smells like ice cream melting on my lover's lips.

Love speaks lots of food, lots of sex, lots of sleep.

Melanin

Levi Tafari

Melanin I love you
you mean so much to me
Oh Melanin your beauty
is far richer than the eye can see
My Melanin embraces me
from my head down to my toe
Oh Melanin I would never forsake you
this I want you to know.

You lie with me
when I sleep at night
You guide me
through the day
You take me to
a higher height
I love to watch
you at play.

I often face heavy abuse
when you're out with me
Some people haven't got my Melanin
so they show their jealousy
But no matter what they say or do
it won't stop me from loving you
My Melanin
precious Melanin
the pigmentation in my skin.

Hour-glass

Saqib Deshmukh

My head is full of you.
My heart is full of you.
My eyes are full of you.
But when our love has gone
Been strangled by the past,
How will I empty
Out this glass?

The Calling

Lemn Sissay

It's a calling love, dark as black ice
As flippant and fraught as loaded dice
We're desperate. How this scorches the eyes
Burrows through the chest, burns into thighs
It's a calling love, the squeal of the whale
Before the slithering harpoon impales
Or the scream of the eagle flaying her wings
At her nest plummeting into the gut of the wind
It's a calling love, a sinister act
The stage is draped in a blanket of black
And there are no words and no direction
Just the imperfect quest for unblemished
    perfection
It's a tangle this, like the first kiss
Thinking is frightening, doing is bliss

Seeds Of Ras Tafari

John Lyons

I

Seven hundred wives and three hundred
   concubines
eclipsed by this dove-eyed queen of the south.
She may have my entire kingdom from Homs
in the north to The Gulf of Aqaba.

Of all the gifts she brought me
none surpasses the promise in her eyes, fishpools
of Heshbon. We shall drink wine from my
   vineyards
in Baalhamon to celebrate, with the rose-purple
spikenard in her hair, the twin pride
of her breasts, her cinnamon-tinted thighs.

No need for the mandrake root. She will come to
   me
in my garden with her phials of fragrant oils
and I will feel her gentleness stir healing
   pleasures.
The land of Judah will have a lion, the temple I
   adorned
with my desire will reverberate with my song of
   songs.

II

The Ethiopian 'Kebra Nagast' claims
that the Queen of Sheba bore Solomon a son.

Through the clamour of his birth celebrations
this lion cub of Judah lay silk-swaddled
in his cradle gazing down the centuries to
    Ras Tafari.

His mewling compelled attention.
He snuggled to his first taste of love.

Rejoicing in his suckle-tug, she recalled that time,
not so long ago, when she entered Solomon's
    garden
with her phials of fragrant oils.

She had lain with her lover among spikenard and
    saffron
under the vaulted ceiling of cedars. And how his
    words
like the spiced wine from the juice of pomegranate
had turned her head to unruly love.

And when he had been sated, emptied of his sap,
she had left him, had taken charge of the future:
the seeds of Ras Tafari.

Love Poem

Saqib Deshmukh

Between the Moon,
The Skies and the Ocean
There is an eternity
Filled by people's dreams.
But not knowing all this
I was conned into thinking
You'd given me the earth.
So as we lay in
Each other's arms
I reached out hungry
For the stars.

September's Song

Jaya Graves

I am rich because you knew me;
drunk on dew
        from a secret spring;
my body clothed in gossamer; fragrant with
oils of jasmine and rose.

Like September am I. Full of the
gifts of many seasons.

I shall give you flame-trees, and
orchards of honey fruit, like those
that grew in Eden, before
Adam forgot.

An amber moon shall shade
our rest. And fields of
        Autumn leaves,
will be our trysting place.

Never

Kosar Saira

Never in my dreams
Could I believe this to be true
Or think the impossible
Our souls dancing in passionate embrace
I dare not imagine your lips
Engulfing my every line

I trembled with the thought
Of your breasts being inside
I lay awake tossing and turning
Every breath screaming, yielding, yearning
For yours to feel
I walked around with your face in my mind
Your eyes burning through my veins

Never did I think your fingers
Would touch my face this way
That your tongue would be
In my mouth, pussy, body
All over

The Crying Rain

Komal Purwaha

I gave you a garland of hearts,
And you gave me a garland of thorns,
I spread flowers for you to walk on,
And you made me dance on glass,
For you I left my family and home,
And you did not give me any respect,
Now where can I go to?
I no longer have a home, and I no
    longer have you,
Where shall I take my love,
I cannot live without respect,
And without your love I cannot live,
My eternal love, do not give me thorns,
    let me soak myself in the rain of
        your love.

Barsaat

Maine tumhe dil ka haar pehenaya,
Tumne mujhe kaanton ka haar diya,
Maine tumhare pairon men phool bechayai,
Aur tumne mujhe kaanch par natchaya,
Tumhare liye maine ghar bar choora,
Aur tumne mujhe eisat nahin de,
Ab hum kahan jahen,

Ghar bar bhi nahin aur tum bhi nahin,
Hum apne pyaar ko liye kahan jahen,
Eisat ke bagayar mein jee nahin sakti,
Aur tumhare pyar ke baghayar mein rehe nahin sakti,
Mere jeevan saathi, mujhe kaante na do
Mujhe pyar ke barsaat men bheig jaane do.

Saturday Night

Saqib Deshmukh

I want you next to me
Your slight body like a gentle
Breeze coming over me
Need to feel your hand in mine
Walking slowly by your side
To your shoreline like the tides

I want you next to me
Your skin so close
It melts to me.
I'm a moth to your inner light
The string pulling to your kite
So I need you here tonight
Oh I need you here tonight.

Your Face, My Heart

Quibilah Montsho

I saw a face today
Which reminded me of the place
Where I first met you
Which reminded me of the time
We first spoke
And my heart was already yours
In cold alleyways and doorways
On park benches and hotel floors
The world stood still
And I tattooed your name on my heart

I saw a face today
Which reminded me
That when you left and took your things
You also took a piece of my heart.

Untitled

John Chombi

I hear the rain fall on the window
a soft, insistent pitter-pat
waking me slow from sleep
deep with thoughts of you
deep with doubts.
Where will we go?
Can we stay together?

The rain turns to snow
the dark clouds take on a subtle glow
I turn to your warmth
and in full waking know
the comfort of your presence.

To My Mother

Tang Lin

When I looking into your eyes
when I looking at your face

I see the shadow
the shadow of my self

You are a woman
a woman to my soul

Wave upon waves
spirit
touching me
haunting me

that you are a woman
a woman to my heart

when I looking into your eyes
when I looking at your face

I see images
images
shadowing you to me

that you are a woman
a woman to my spirit

You gave life
you gave birth
you offer yourself

You are a woman
a woman that I love

You are a woman
a woman
You are my mother
my mother
You are a woman
a woman that I love
you are my mother

Something In The Air

Seni Seneviratne

There's something
in the air
between us
you said
makes it difficult
to talk
about anything

At least that's
something
I thought
I was beginning
to feel like
there's nothing
between us
any more

and the moon on the water
was moving with the ripples
and everything we said
kept moving on
in circles

8 am

Milan Ghosh

Sunday morning arrives
Winter, crisp blues
Grey twilight pall
Bay window view in soul mirror.

I danced 'til three last night.
Jiving, rocking, twisting hips,
Hoping you'd appear.
Walked home
On the glittering, streetlit
Frosty iced pavements,
Winding my way home.
4 am in bed. I'm dead.
Waking early as usual
Fitful sleep, restless
Like a suffocating fish.
Finally decided to get up.
Sad, sad Sunday lover's blues.

Snatched Moments

Frances Rahman

Every afternoon we meet
Time spent together
Shrouded in deceit.

Where will all this end
When in public, stiff and polite
We act as though you're my distant friend.

I want to shout and declare you as my lover
Would your wife, my husband
Ever believe that we could both love one another.

Let us enjoy each little time
When I am truly yours
And that moment you are truly mine.

Sincerity And Innocence

Tang Lin

You came
to my dream
in distant

With your tender
tendering smile
With your eye
like the star shining
in the night

Embracing love
calling the soul to arise
the spirit to rejoice
the heart zest with happiness

Soaring above
silver rain falling
gold orangeish red sunset
river float   river float

Melt melt away
sorrow sadness hate
hurt pain hardness

You came to my dream
in distant

With your tender
tendering smile
With your eye
like the star shining
in the night

My spirit
rushing to your smile
naked
pure sincere   innocence
overflow with loving enthusiasm

You came
to my dreams
in distant

Throw Your Love Away

Mei-Chi Chan

And like feathered snow,
Let it fall ... *Lightly*,
On mountain slopes of peppery pine,
Valleys unfurling patchwork textures,
Wet roof tiles lit with sunlight,
A wood-latticed window, open,
Charcoal flames scouring blackened pots,
And on this hard dirt floor

Watch it melt.

Love And Lust

Milan Ghosh

How you walk, and talk
How you smile
You beguile me
How you laugh and giggle.

You delight and excite me
Make me yearn
Make me full of desire.
Passionate and gentle - tender,
Or both together. Understand?

Eastern Senses

Selina Deen

As she walks the folds of her sari whisper,
'Look at me, see me, hear me.'
Her eyes are lowered to the ground,
But I can hear the whisper of her sari.

The smell intoxicates, the aromas are carried on
    the breeze,
And remain in the tresses of her long, black hair.
As she walks the aroma beckons,
'Look at me, see me, hear me.'
And I can see and hear her Eastern senses.

Next Time

Seni Seneviratne

I was a desert
shut tight against
the winds of nostalgia
until you came
in an African winter
beating at my hearts drum
to let you in from the cold
I thought your body
would turn to dust
like the lover
in my dreams
but your skin
was warm
flowing
through my hands
covering every inch of me
watering my dry
making all my
passion
flowers
bloom

T.

Zareen Zahid Hussain

washing henna
onto
bruised hands
whilst
soaking tears
into
a used Kleenex

as

her lover
waits
in
his
father's car,
across
the street,
letting
the engine run

desperate

to
keep

love alive.

You Can't Catch It By Kissing

Tina Tamsho

When I finally believed
you were HIV Positive,
I Kissed you on the mouth,
Kissed you full on the Lips;
And then you Kissed me
on my mouth,
on my Lips,
And then we laughed
And Kissed each other again
on the mouth
And on the Lips
And all we gave each other
was our Love,
our friendship,
our sensitivity,
and most of all,
Our INTELLIGENCE.
NO YOU CAN'T CATCH IT BY KISSING,
But Kissing a Friend
Can help to break down
IGNORANCE!

The Kissing Ritual

John Siddique

I came in here to experience coolness
in this summertime.
and to write yesterday's words
which are.

It's one of those days
when my eyelids need kissing
for your bottom lip to cut the dryness.
so I may breathe out longly.
To find the shifting light on my knee
filtering down through wind-blown leaves.

On the lawn red bottomed honeybees
discover clover.
An inactive green space is not what it seems.

It teems with life when I bother to look.

This is fine
but it doesn't stop me feeling so horny
I could crack a walnut
between my thighs.

Hands

SuAndi

If I hold your hand like so...
Not so, / like two friends shopping.
Or so, / like mother and child
Leading, caring, chastising,
If I hold your hand like so...

See, how the two palms meet like hearts beating.
And the fingers entwine like two bodies lying
If I hold your hand like so.

In India everyone holds hands.
Men with women
Women with women,
And men with men.
So.
If I hold your hand like so,
                         Will you think me perverse.

Celtic Knots

Maya Chowdhry

she takes the thread
i listen to belonging
makan
zamin
ghar
between her fingers
three times
come
listen
touch
i swim in breath
and rest my fingers
on her lips
three times
pani
samudr
hava
she ties the thread
three times
wide
hand
after
around my wrist
my fingers slip
into
her
mouth

into the knot
she sucks
wet
skin
open
the thread lies
on a large stretch
of belonging
between
my
skin
and
hers

The Poet's Song

Pete Kalu

Some people talk about New York, New York,
London and its Tower Bridge, the mangoes
of sweet Trinidad, but me?

I love Moss Side

Some people talk about trifle with double
cream waking up in waterbeds with their
toyboys/lovers, but me?

I love Moss Side

Some people nibble ears, hold hands all
day, give each other fluffy bears, steam
up car windows sucking toes n stuff, but me?

I love Moss Side

Some people go dippy at fresh pink flowers some
spend their time dreaming of filmi stars,
some rave about Daleks and cable TV, but me?

I love Moss Side
"   "   "   "
"   "   "   "

Heart, Don't Break...

Komal Purwaha

We love one person,
And marry another,
For our parents' happiness
   this is the way
To love from the heart,
   my friend may I never
      make that mistake:

Dil Na Toote

Pyaar ek se karna
Aur shadi kisi aur se,
Maa, Baap ki khushi ke liye
yehi hai dastoor,
Pyaar dil se karna, mere dost
 hum kabhie na karhen yeh
      bhool.

Kissing Asians

Saqib Deshmukh

I had a thought once...
Blimey Saqib my old son
You never see Asians kissing
Do ya?
Then I thought more carefully...
Y'see,
Expressions of affection
Might be part of your code,
But expressions of love
Are one different thing though.
A kiss can be cold and callous,
An embrace too smothering,
Love is more than just affection.
It's about respect and dignity.
So next time
I see Kevin snogging,
Or Lucy necking Pete
I will snigger
'Cos my Asian secret's here
And goes everywhere with me.
'Cos my love will not be
A prison sentence
My love will set me free.
And the lack of
Kissing Asians
Will not be strange to me.

For Love's Sake

SuAndi

I want to write love poetry
So touch me here,
Where it hurts to inspire me.

Don't blow in my ear
That only chills me.
Touch me here,
Where it hurts to inspire me.

Please don't ruffle my hair,
And try to embrace not grapple with me.
And could you remove that stubble that you call a beard
Before you attempt to kiss me.

Take your elbow out of my back
And why are your knees so knobbly.
Did you know what you call muscles are really fat
And balding does nothing for me.

I can't write with feelings cold
Come put your arms around
And touch me where it hurts
Honey, why are you choking me.

The Edge

Maya Chowdhry

Kismet is
one essence
smells sweet
tastes like pleasure
I touch fate
lick the edges
of her look.

Cherries

Maya Chowdhry

december freezes my
nipples they stand hard
and cold, she plucks them
ripe, squeezes and sucks, I
fall beneath her holding
her waist, heavy breath
and kiss. I press my
face to her soft
belly and begin.

It is cold, she is hot I
slide right in, Strawberry Avenue
heat sizzling, she moves on
my hand, I slide and sigh, she
gasps, further until my hand is
a pineapple growing she opens, I
catch her look, draw her in whole,
move her hair from her face, want
her wild, want her wet in
my palm, flowing deep and long,
the ganges a long way off,
I am in her, her purple heart flowing
I want a place there, faraway
San Francisco love, the heart of a
woman to warm December
in england.

That - You And Me

Kosar Saira

That look in your eyes
When we were making love
That juice on your lips
Dripped like a waterfall
Into my mouth

That touch of your hand
Felt so strong
Yet so gentle

That feel of your locks
Covering my face
Like a blanket
From the world outside

That sweat that poured from our bodies
Like a river in our dreams
That noise of your
Each breath, sigh, yearning, moaning
Movement of body, mind and soul

That neverending feeling
Of sheer happiness, contentment and satisfaction

That desire for your
Every touch, look, smell
The whole of you

That neverending second, minute, hour
We spent together
That time in time

The appreciation
Of you, me, ourselves together
That beautiful view
Of your sheer blackness
The magnificence of Africa and Asia
Both of us together

That forever desire
Of making love
Being with you
Feeling you
From your feet to your head
To the inside of your legs to your mouth

That
Thirst for only you

The Sweet Smell Of Success

Lorraine Scott

The sweet smell of freshly
fallen raindrops on the
dusty tarmac roads.
strawberries.
the sweet smell of freshly
made love in the early
hours of day.
Carnations.
The sweet smell of freshly
washed sheets in the
place of rest.
Baking.
The sweet smell of freshly
born babies lying in
their cribs.
The sweet smell of my
loved one lying close to me
his body, his life
and his breathing.

Sunset

Samir Chatterjee

You wanted to stay.
In this many splendoured world
Which you only felt through dense smoke,
Simply stared from a worn-out glass:
Your debt no one can repay.

You desired to love.
The night pined for the stars;
Sky was betrothed to the sea.
A river thrusting its way to the ocean:
You filled the horizon with doves.

They came from all corners.
Weaning them on your tender milk,
Building their muscles with your sweat
You grew until the very branches of the tree
Became the plant's own carcass.

In earnest began the retrieval show
They did not nurse you while you were young;
In the battlefield you were left bleeding.
Your sunset took a long time to die
Filling the universe with a sinking glow.

Your pain breathes fire!
Among the dying embers your last letter
Was not read. The parched papyrus

In twisted black smoke did not raise false alarms:
Under the ash were buried all desires.

Smile

Na Oyo Quartey

Smile for me, go on, I love it,
When you smile your eyes light up,
There's a glow in your face,
And a dimple in your cheek.

It shows me you're happy,
Shows you're pleased to see me,
Makes me feel kinda special,
Sorta shows your love.

When you go away you smile,
A sad sort of smile,
Which tugs at my heart,
Shows you'll miss me.

If you're not with me,
I remember your smile,
It reminds me of you,
Forever in my mind.

Whenever I'm lonely,
Your face I see,
And the smile that I love
Is as special as you are to me.

A Cup Of You

Scorcha

I was alone, drunk,
in sorrow, no life
no love, no vision,
then, just a taste
of you, sobered me
in joy.

With eyes now open,
I see and applaud,
your sweet lips,
that whisper songs
to my heart cord,
um!
I feel rhythms of
love for you.

Arise and stand in
perfection, let me
admire your creation
Black woman,
I embrace your rich
body in comfort,
I honour the display
of your mind's pictures,
I'm alive and with it
because of your spirit.

I adore your flow of
grace, as you weave the
womanhood of our race,
You hold the core of
every heart's core,
I'm filled with you
and want no more.

Love's Blow

John Chombi

In the first full flush
Base bodily functions are denied
Lips greedily kissed
Are never pictured having a piss.
That rounded, shapely bottom
Gives vent to rotten smells
But such foulness goes forgotten
Memory never tells.

Romance's bloom withers
Notice the bad breath?
Recognising the reek of garlic
Signals young love's death.

Look At The Weather

Timothy Wesley

Now she shows him the proof of her life,
as the rain begins to flood from her eyes
she's hurt as he moves towards that flood
it was murky so he swam around two filled holes
that can't be denied

And after it's all been soaked up
He finds that he too has those eyes.

Have You Ever Felt The Breeze

Lorraine Scott

Have you ever felt the breeze
gently stroke your cheekbone?

Have you ever felt the breeze,
quietly brush over your hair,
kissing every strand along the way?

Have you ever felt the breeze
send a tingle up your spine?

Have you ever felt the breeze
moving through the trees?

I have felt the breeze,
when you are close to me.

Veneer

Rodney Taylor

I want you.
    Each dream is molested by your caresses.

I want you.
    I care for you in your ignorance' of the truth.

I want you.
    There is a thin veneer in between me and U.

I Never Can Say Goodbye

Quibilah Montsho

Why so hard to say goodbye?
Never again to glimpse your eye?
Never to feel your sweet skin touch
My head, my breasts, my lips so much
One more hug, one more squeeze
Still my soul and let me breathe
Your skin, your eyes, your lips,
Your breasts, your stomach, your fingertips
Why so hard to say goodbye?
Please, one more lustful, licking sigh.

Forbidden Love

Aaron Rouse

In the night the passion swells -
Of sweet cologne, your body smells.
I stroke the orbs, shaped like bells.
A secret love of which - we dare not tell -
Into this fountain we both gladly fell.

Sweetly, gently, I kissed your lips -
Sucking, sensuously, your fingertips.
Your lingerie slowly slips.
As we dress, the guilt grips -
Forbidden love's peaks and dips.

'Round your body, the linen folds,
Love denied this night, we two hold.
Warm inside, outside the snow is cold.
You whisper 'My lover should be told.'
For me, just love on the dole -
You have given your soul.

We breathe so deep, we breathe in time -
Down the Lane the church bells chime.
Bodies in motion - move in rhyme -
Near the street with trees of lime.
In the room, the temperature - climbs.
A feeling divine, A motion sublime.

Emotion

Victoria McKenzie

I experience the feeling that makes me
want to open my mouth and speak
words spring from my emotion
when I say I love you
you ought to know I want you

But if I make you aware of
my feelings
your reaction might give me
blunt information about myself

I am afraid of your silences
of what it could mean
and I talk to you because
I want you to know how I feel
I don't want to listen to just
what you say I want your
loving feelings

Tell me the way you see it
rather than the way it is
then this will help me to
discover fully of the way
I see it both body and soul.

Final Demand

Elaine Okoro

Words:
    I fancy you
    Like
    Want = demanding?
Craving for an interlock session that doesn't feel
    like the bell
going for a wrestling match.

Feelings:
    Enjoyment
    Pleasure
    Desiring
Even wanting a little bit more; that just
doesn't mean a day!

Denying feelings
    losing respect
Finding confusion in words, feelings
that are never spoken.

Anger:
    Don't tell me there isn't anymore
for who? you? me?
    Where is the sharing beyond the
bodies that leads to - ? Caring thoughts,
consideration about my feelings.

Ending:
    Goodbye   Fuck off
      Take care   Love you.

Lust + Love = Forever

Gloria Knowles

It's instilled in me that misshaped face.
The thinning hair and close set eyes,
Separated only just, by a nose.
A lustful mouth hovering on the verge of
    seduction.
Those outstretched hands, so femininely
Soft and ready to gently explore.
Familiar sounds of cooing and cawing; the mating,
Yes this love game begins.
Sweat, perspiration or just animal
Magnetism causes a revolution amongst flesh.
A cemented bond is achieved in seconds to
Cast away thoughts of frustration.
Then isn't love all in all destined to grow?

Roaring Lion

Paulette Browne

My man is like a roaring lion
His mane does reach his waist
He is the king of the forest
No other man could ever take his place

I am his queen and he is my king
Together we will reign
And love will be our anthem
And everybody will sing

To Jah be the glory for ever and ever
For bringing us two people together
And what Jah has joined together
Let no man put asunder

When my man moves everyone looks
No one could match his agility
No one could match his love

He indeed is the king of the forest
And the king of my heart
And where love is
Freedom shall never part.

Love

Trudy Blake

Love is
Foaming waves
Calmness of the sea
The setting sun
It's orange glow
Like a sunflower.

The blue of the sky
Foaming clouds
Dancing together
A summer breeze
To cool my red
Hot passion.

Raindrops trickling
Down
Diamonds from
The sky
That make the
Flowers grow

Bees, insects,
All earthly
And heavenly
Things combine
A look,
A touch

That money won't
Buy, the care
Of a friend
In time of
Need.
That
Is
Love.

To Love You

Prince Marley

To love you is to experience a happiness
That destroys the bridges to hurt
And establishes a distance to heartbreak

To love you promotes the feelings
of togetherness forever
and creates the opportunity

to liaise with passion

to love you extinguishes the
fire of loneliness
presenting in its place a
new warmth
that is comparable to the
sunshine

to love you is a dream with
a touch of reality
the dawning of a new day
that floats around and
slowly obliterates the darkness
that once clouded my life.

Integration

Frances Rahman

Is our love really wrong
Do you sometimes get confused
And wonder where you belong.

If we have children will it confuse
Both our cultures must be adopted
This they must not lose.

My father shouted,
'But my dear don't forget you're Muslim
What about your traditions, religion
Do you really love HIM

What will our family and friends think
Do YOU have to bring about integration
Acting and creating the missing link.'

The wedding will hopefully bring about the two
If they can't overcome their prejudice
Just remember
I LOVE YOU.

Found

Shamsa Butt

When you
Have found yourself
You
Have found love.

The Fat Man's Song

Pete Kalu

I am big an I am fat
An I like a woman who is like that!

I wan someone who can carry spare tyre
Like opera singer or woman town crier

I am big an I am fat
An I like a woman who is like that

When in bed we'll shake an rock
Till de springs go bung-a-dung doing-boing bok!

I am big an I am fat
An I like a woman who is like that

Big is beautiful big is huge
big is generous, not a scrooge

If mi han get aroun yuh, mi doan wan fe know
Cause I like a woman who cyaan see her toe!

I am big an I am fat
An I like a woman who is like that

If you think this woman is you
Well I'll be loving to all of you!

When Spirit Moved

Tang Lin

The surreal of water in the lake
reflects the deepest of my heart
which is beautiful and real

The sunlight split
dark and bright

For this moment
I was in the shades
feeling belonging and emptying my thoughts

For the next moment
I was in the light
bathing the sunlight
creating words to describe
my emotions and love

A butterfly
orange and black colour
flapping its wings
rested on a white trainer

I thought
it was beautiful

Shower of thoughts
gathering my spirit

I was alone
walking in the field of joy

I dance
my spirit compose
and my soul sings

My body moves
in curves of landscape
waves of ocean

My voice sings
sound of beauty

My soul celebrate
being and living for I

Once again
the realm of love vibrating in me

Perfume

Saqib Deshmukh

I do not know
whether I saw you
In a dream or not.
But there was something
in the air...
As soon as I heard
your name
You were there...

Kushboo

Muja nahin patta hai
maina apko dekhata
quarb mai or nahin
Laikeen Havar mai
Kutch ta....
Jessa maina apka
narm soonnah
os jugga mai
arp tain.

Shadows

Jaya Graves

In the breeze against my cheek,
I feel you. And I hear you
in the silence of the trees.

Yet shadows hide your face
as surely as the vision that
lures you
beyond my reach.

You came ... so slow ...
insidious as sunset turning dusk
to take the core of me
from my own keeping.

Only in the
cry of seagulls sweeping seaward
now I hear you.

Quibilah (East African name meaning harmony)

Kosar Saira

Quibilah I love you
from your pussy to your face
from your arms to your legs
from your eyes to your nose
from your armpits to your locks
from your backside to your front
from your fingers to your toes
from your cheeks to your knees
from your eyebrows to your ears
from your nipples to your belly button
from your spine to your ankle
from your foot to your gut

Avenue

Maya Chowdhry

Blue, I turn cold beneath
the sheets, turn to you and I
burn like the august sun. sweet
sweat runs and pours and I want to
pour, april rain into you.

Beyond the blue,
the red and gold wedding of distance.
I want to hold, beyond the blue. I
return to yellow sand, burns
my feet red,
the golden grains gathering
my heat grows.

She is a pirate and I smuggle
gold for her.
she journeys oceans and returns
to me. I give her rubies and she
gives me honey and watermelon, I am
sweet in the heat
and do not feel the sand
burning my feet. Red
and the blue
disappears to black.

I dream of her in Barcelona,
Avenue Portal de l'angel,

from the shimmer of the street she rises.
She is september, october, november, december
blue. And I am
blue. Mediterranean blue,
like the sea.

Purple Heart

Seni Seneviratne

I am lazy as the Zambesi
drifting, treading water
just around the corner
maybe there'll be
the rushing
            roaring
                      falling
the juice of the mango
to curl my tongue around.
My heart has grown
purple with longing
but July comes and goes
each year and still
no lover paints
her pleasure on my skin.

Some nights she comes
and seasons my dreams
finds me in Colombo streets
leaves the print of her hand
in my palm
the curve of her skin
on my back
the breath of her kiss
on my neck
but always her face
escapes me

When morning comes
I bathe in the memories
and drift on
lazy waiting.

Marriage

SuAndi

The next man I meet I am going to marry
Do not think me impetuous
Or foolhardy
Marry in haste
Has always been a bad omen
I have heeded every warning
Virtuous woman always comes out tops
Yet I have been on top, lots
Good girls grow to be better
My behaviour is merited in gold letters
For forty years I have tarried
So now you know why
The next man I meet
                    I'm going to marry

If You Leave

SuAndi

If you leave me
I will not rip out my hair.
Disgrace myself by weeping in public.
Lose weight.
Unfortunately.
Tell anyone willing to listen
Of our most intimate moments.
If you leave,
Inside me there will be a void.
That will ache
And ache
And ache.

Again

Deyika Nzeribe

Again
We meet
And talk
And joke
And smile
And stop
Just short of kisses
And part
Again.

Culture And Assimilation

Shamsa Butt

We express our love
Through Ancient conventions
Laid down by culture.
If we assimilate
Then
We express no love at all.

Labouring Lost Love

Sua Huab

The first time we kissed
I melted.
The last time
I thought you smelt
Of cigarettes.

Change Not Blame

Sua Huab

Once
you loved me just as I
was

now
you love me as I
was -
then.

In A New Land

Mei-Chi Chan

Silence sings between the notes
Of the morning chorus
Mountains tumble wild
Upwards to the sky
The still green lake
Cups my vision in its bowl
A steady breeze moves softly
From the past

How far must I travel
Not to hear your call?

Splitting Up

Mei-Chi Chan

This shore, the body of my soul,
You have flowed over, grain by grain.
I am flooded with you,
Infused with your essence,
Soaked to saturation...
You have bound me to you,
Made us one.

All the time the moon was dying,
The tides turned never to return.

Biographies

SuAndi
Performance Poet and Live Artist, SuAndi has been performing nationally and internationally since 1985. 'I long resisted writing love poetry. I was busy dealing with The Issues. Then I met love. I didn't fall in love, but it made me realise how wonderful and infuriating the whole business is. Love wandered away, yet I am still writing.'

Trudy Blake
I am a performer and singer. I was born in Jamaica and came to England in the Sixties, and worked in factories packing. I also did tailoring. I started to write poetry and songs when I joined a creative writing group. I write about things I see. My poems have been broadcast on Radio 5, and I have performed all over the North West.

Paulette Browne
Paulette Browne is a twenty-eight year old woman. 'My parents were born in St Kitts and Nevis, places where culture, warmth and beautiful people abound, and where I found an appreciation of who I was. This has led me to express myself

today through the words of a poem. Tomorrow, who knows!'

Shamsa Butt
True poetry must deal with the ultimate questions of truth, value and the purpose of life. These truths should be expressed in the simplest and clearest language. Only depth of thought should shine through the words of the poem. This inspires my poetry. Only such poetry can help the oppressed.

Mei-Chi Chan
Mei-Chi Chan was born in Hong-Kong and lived in Nigeria between the age of two and eight before being transplanted to England. She is a philosophy graduate and spent three years teaching TEFL, writing and publishing TEFL materials in Taiwan. She is presently a Creative Writing Liaison Officer for Liverpool Libraries.

Debjani Chatterjee
Indian born Debjani Chatterjee is a poet, prose writer and storyteller. Her poetry collections are: *I Was That Woman* and *The Sun Rises In The North*. Recent books include: *The Monkey God* and *Sufi Stories From Around The World*. She has co-edited two bilingual anthologies: *Barbed Lines* and *Sweet and Sour*.

Samir Chatterjee
I grew up in a steel township in India. I came to the UK to train in management accountancy, but gave it up and never went back. After studying sociology at the LSE I worked in the community development field in Coventry, Norfolk, Liverpool and Rochdale. I retired early from Rochdale Council as a Principal Community Education Officer in 1993.

John Chombi
John Chombi, 38, lives in Salford with his wife and two children. He was born in Jamaica and came to England at the age of 10. He went to school in Manchester and it was while at secondary school that he had his first poem published on BBC radio. He is now a trained journalist working in broadcast television.

Maya Chowdhry
Maya Chowdhry is a poet, film-maker and performance poet. She was a winner of the BBC Radio Young Playwrights Festival with *Monsoon*, (published by Aurora Metro Publications), and of the Cardiff International Poetry Competition. Her poetry is collected in *Putting in the Pickle where the Jam Should Be* and she has contributed to numerous anthologies.

Selina Deen
Selina Deen is a prolific writer of poetry and short

stories, and an avid reader of Crocus publications. Her writing is topical and accessible.

Saqib Deshmukh

Saqib Deshmukh was born in South London in 1967. After a few years as a kid he developed into a writer and downwardly mobile political activist. After plying his trade in London he left the Big Smoke for Manchester where he met Lemn Sissay and, well, the rest is history... He is currently living it up with Aajkal theatre as resident writer and worker and' has been working with THE KALIPHZ.

Milan Ghosh

Winner of Preston Other Paper's 1990 poetry competition, Milan Ghosh has been writing for many years. Milan describes himself as 'a (black and) blue member of the lumpen proletariat'. He is an avid student and reads widely. The poem, *Rika* was inspired by a Herman Hesse poem which he read in 'a small yellow paperback which someone nicked years ago!'

Jaya Graves

Born - long ago. Location - India. Gender - female. Status - divorced. Three kids (worth cloning!). Grandchild. Lovely parents. One passed over. Interests - politics/poetry. Potent mixture. Concerns - 'Third' World. Injustice.

Oppression. Work - questioning these. Ambition- challenging status quo. Working with others, to shift balance. Beliefs/value system - we are powerful. We can change things. Let's do it!

Sua Huab

I am twenty four years old and originally from Wigan. I left to live in Leeds in 1987, moved to Manchester in 1990 and for the past two years have lived and worked in Liverpool. I'm interested in Black feminist politics and have been writing on and off for ten years. Previous publications include *Black and Priceless* and *Talkers Through Dream Doors*.

Zareen Zahid Hussain

...21, an undergraduate, and I've been writing seriously since moving to Manchester over 3 years ago... That's about it really. I'm too young to be writing biographies.

Pete Kalu

In 1990 Pete hammered out *Afrogoth* for Radio Four. Top-ranking black fiction publishers, X-Press, published his first novel, the urban thriller, *Lick Shot* in November 1993. He finds poetry a catalyst for his general writing skills. His ambition is to win the Nobel Prize for Literature.

Gloria Knowles
Born in the West Midlands thirty years ago from Jamaican parents. Wrote for Wolverhampton Radio's 'Thought For The Day' programme. Received in 1988 a special 'Livewire Award' for business enterprise in Blackpool. Her work has been published in *Talkers Through Dream Doors*, *De Homeplace*, and *Contemporary Verse 1992*.

Muhammad Khalil Eugene Lange
Muhammad Khalil Eugene Lange is a jazz griot, teacher and writer. In 1980 he was awarded a Black Penmanship Award from A.C.E.R. for an essay on Rasta. He collaborated with performer Levi Tafari to form Oduduwa Black Performing Arts Co-op. His recordings include *The Ministry of Love* with Levi Tafari, *Urban Jahz*, *Naffi Locksman*, *Bugs on the Wire*, and *Sir Freddies Hi-Power HiFi*. He currently performs with the Blackamoors.

John Lyons
John Lyons is a poet and painter; three-times Peterloo Poets prizewinner, he has also received an Arts Council Bursary for poetry. He has read his work on TV and radio. Publications include *Lure of the Cascadura*, *The Sun Rises In The North*, *New British Poetry*. He has exhibited nationally and internationally as a painter.

Prince Marley

Prince Marley aka Donald Stewart was born in 1956, the son of George Stewart and Mabel Stewart, local fisherman and schoolteacher. He came to live in England in 1970. He started writing at the tender age of twelve, and won Gold in Jamaica's Speech Festival 1989 for his poem, HUNGER. He has performed in the USA, Japan, and Canada. He is a self-educated poet. His nickname Marley is because of his message lyrics.

Cheryl Martin

Born in Washington DC, Cheryl graduated in 1986 from Emmanuel College, Cambridge and is currently finishing a Ph.D. The adopted Mancunian has won grants from the Arts Council and North West Playwrights, the 1990 Cultureword Poetry Prize, residencies at Contact Theatre and Pit Prop Theatre, with poems published in *The Sun Rises In The North* (Smith/Doorstop Press).

Quibilah Montsho

Quibilah is a poet, writer, performer and workshop facilitator, currently living and working in Manchester. She has performed her work widely across the country, is currently working on her first novel and likes to describe herself as a political black lesbian of African descent, whose work has to be experienced to be believed.

Victoria McKenzie
Victoria writes in English and Creole language. She has had numerous poems published and read her work on radio, in schools, colleges and theatres. She runs writing workshops for adults and children.

Deyika Nzeribe
My life in 50 words or less? (7). Perhaps: I've been writing poetry for a while now and I guess I like it. I also like coffee, Summer, 'Rugrats', friends, family. (30). Or maybe: 27, Black, single, seeks life and more than 50 words in which to tell it. (50).

Elaine Okoro
I am a Black female who has produced two children amongst other creative work. Of African-Jamaican parentage with a dash of Irish, I am African in mind and spirit. I was brought up and born in England- July 19th 1960- Cancerian.

Komal Purwaha
The poems I write are about feelings and pain. These are written, not thought of. I thank my mother who inspired me to write, again. Thanks to Anjli who supported me. Thanks also to my family of friends in London. All my poems are dedicated to my late father, Mr Som Dutt Purwaha.

Na Oyo Quartey
My cultural heritage is African/Ghanaian father and Lancashire/Bolton mother. I am 42, a single parent with three children and have been writing since my teens. In the last ten years I have been writing for performance and publication.

Frances Rahman
Frances Rahman, of Bangladeshi origin, was born and lives in Liverpool. She began taking her writing seriously after becoming involved in an Asian writers workshop. She writes poetry, short stories and performs monologues. Frances mainly writes comedy as she feels that she is able to convey strong messages through humour.

Aaron Rouse
I am 29 years old and started writing poetry in December 1992. An acquaintance showed me one of his poems and I decided to try it. I produced three poems. People who read my poetry liked my style, which encouraged me to continue. Now I get commissions to write poems for friends.

Kosar Saira
Kosar Saira is a black (Pakistani, Mirpuri) lesbian who works in a number of media in her spare time, including the short story, poetry, photography and film. Her work has been published in the United States as well as in this

country. Kosar works for the Law Centres Federation and is reading Law.

Scorcha
I found a rhythm for poetry through Cultureword. I checked out a writing weekend at Lumb Bank. Respect to Jack Mapanje and Tina Tamsho who led the way for my solid foundation at Lumb Bank. Pete Kalu and all concerned, respect is due to the maximum. Marie Evans, your poem showed me all the necessaries for 'A Cup Of You.'

Lorraine Scott
I was born in Newcastle Upon Tyne and grew up in some of the toughest towns. I have been writing from a very early age from a Black Geordie perspective. As well as poetry, I write short stories, essays and have had one book review published in *Feminist Arts News*. I recently graduated from Sunderland Polytechnic with a Certificate in Youth and Community Work. I moved to Manchester in 1992.

Seni Seneviratne
I was born in Yorkshire to an English mother and Sri Lankan father. I am a writer and singer who recently branched out into photography and I combine all three for performance. I run regular writing workshops for women as part of my work in Adult Education in Sheffield, where I

live with my teenage daughter.

John Siddique
B Born 25 July 1964
I Integrity - the most important virtue
O Over and above into love
G Gold light of the sun (I wish the rain would stop)
R Roses
A A.J. - My beautiful son
P (Self) Publicist...I am that thing
H Heaven is within our reach
Y Your respect.

Lemn Sissay
I visited earth in 1967 and decided it would be useful to stick around. Got a flat in HulmeZone2 Number 27. Friends tell me that I am Out To Lunch, I tell them, no, I am Lemn Sissay and I love fried chicken that's what I love.

Levi Tafari
Levi Tafari is a crucial, rhythmic, poetic, consciousness raiser and urban griot from Liverpool. As a writer and performer Levi has worked locally, nationally and internationally. Levi has had collections of his work published and his plays performed. Levi works with many artists from different art forms and various

media, ie TV, radio, stage, etc, injecting his work into these. His style is rhythmic and lyrical and has the ability to make you smile and to make you think.

Tina Tamsho
Tina Tamsho is an honours graduate in General Arts, and has special qualifications in Recreational Arts For The Community. Publications include *Blackwomen Talk Poetry*, *The Common Thread*, and *Blackscribe Poetry*. She has recently compiled her first collection of poetry entitled *I Am The Land*, to be published in 1994. Tina teaches Drama and facilitates interdisciplinary workshops.

鄧蓮 Tang Lin
I was born in a village called 'Yung Shu O' 榕樹澳 hidden in the shadow of Hong Kong. My mother speaks Cantonese, my father speaks Hakka, I speak Cantonese, Hakka, Mandarin and English, and I write Chinese and English. I enjoy thinking about hopes and turning them into present times.

Rodney Taylor
I am an African, anarchist love poet. Shock! (You never guessed it, eh!) Born in Manchester, I am tri-cultural, and bi. I enjoy/endure writing and I am trying to be a poet.

Timothy Wesley

Most people who like to write prefer to be under cover and low profile... not me. I want all the trappings, the gloss and the glamour. Forget about morals and right on-ism. In an un-glib stance, I love to enjoy life.

About Cultureword and Commonword

Cultureword was established in 1986 as a Centre for Black creative writing in the North West. Since that time it has achieved rapid success in discovering, developing and promoting Black writers.

Cultureword works across the spectrum of writing forms. Its development work takes in page and performance poetry, short stories, playwrighting, writing for radio, TV and video, and novel-writing.

Cultureword also organises performances, workshops, residencies, lectures, courses and seminars. It provides a manuscript reading service for North West writers and co-ordinates a Writers Agency.

Black writers associated with Cultureword have achieved local, regional and national prominence in their chosen fields.

Cultureword is a part of the vibrant, North West community publishers, Commonword. Commonword seeks to encourage the creative writing and publishing of the diverse groups in society who have lacked, or been excluded from this means of expression. Black writers, women, disabled people, and lesbians and gay men all too often fall into this category.

Crocus is the imprint for books published by

Commonword and Cultureword. *Kiss* is the sixteenth title to be published under the Crocus imprint.

Commonword is supported by: the Association of Greater Manchester Authorities, North West Arts Board and Manchester Education Committee.

The Commonword offices are at Cheetwood House, 21 Newton Street, Manchester M1 1FZ. Our phone number is (061) 236 2773. We would like to hear from you.

Recent Crocus titles

Crocus Five Women Poets
A showcase of poetry by Barbara Bentley, Marguerite Gazeley, Francis Nagle, Sheila Parry and Pat Winslow. These five women are quickly emerging as some of the North West's most talented poets.
'Here are poems that tackle everything from domestic chores to international politics with grace, wit and assurance.' (*Steve Waling, City Life*)
ISBN 0 946745 16 1
Price £5.95 Pbk

Dancing on Diamonds
Poetry and short stories from thirty-six young writers. Lively and provocative.
'The past revisited, the future seen with hopeful vision and the anger of the innocent. A collection of contemporary thoughts by a new breed of contemporary writers - a real pleasure.' (*Art Malik*)
ISBN 0 946745 06 4
Price £5.95 Pbk

The Delicious Lie
This book marks the arrival of a fresh, highly talented new voice onto the British poetry scene.
'What a wonderful, wonderful slice of love and life this is. A gorgeous, scrumptious piece of poetic justice from new(ish) writer Georgina

Blake.' (Nayaba Aghedo, City Life)
ISBN 0 946745 07 2
Price £4.95 Pbk

Rainbows In The Ice
This book of poetry demonstrates the wealth of creative talent that exists within the disabled community. A unique and memorable collection.
'An impressive anthology... It's good to read poets who remember that expressing and eliciting emotion are the centrepieces of writing effective poetry.' (Robert Hamberger, Mailout)
'A lovely collection of poetry by some highly talented people.' (Jackie Glatter, Mencap News)
ISBN 0 946745 90 0
Price £4.50 Pbk

A Matter of Fat (First Edition)
This incisive and humorous novel follows the fortunes of Stella, the leader of 'Slim-Plicity', a commercial slimming club, and some of the club members. When a Fat Women's Support Group starts up nearby, complications soon follow...
'In A Matter of Fat, Ashworth has retained a wicked sense of humour, while raising some very important questions.' (New Woman)
'Sherry Ashworth writes with wit, compassion, excruciating honesty, and controlled, creative anger.' (Zoe Fairbairns, Everywoman)
ISBN 0 946745 95 1
Price £4.95 Pbk

Flame
A dual language book of poetry in English and Urdu by Asian writers. Love, home life, racism and other political issues are some of the areas explored by the fifteen talented poets in *Flame*. Translations are by Alishan Zaidi.
'One of the best collections of Asian poetry I have read.' (Kam Kaur, Eastern Eye)
'Powerful and distinctive...a pleasure to read.' (Shelley Khair, Yorkshire Artscene)
ISBN 0 946745 85 4
Price £4.50 Pbk

Herzone
Fantasy short stories by women. Ranging from science fiction, to 'twist in the tale' stories and mythical fantasies, this collection has something to delight and entertain everyone.
'There is nothing but pleasure to be gained from these tales.' (Manchester Evening News)
'A varied and satisfying collection.' (Zoe Fairbairns, Everywoman)
ISBN 0 946745 80 3
Price £4.50 Pbk

Beyond Paradise
An original collection of poetry that celebrates the vitality of gay and lesbian writing. Provocative, funny and touching, *Beyond Paradise* offers fresh perspectives on life in the '90s - and beyond!
'I promise you, once you've read it, you'll keep coming back for another little glimpse of life

in the lesbian and gay lane.'(Scene Out)
'The tragic nature of human existence, the fun and joy of being alive are here...' (Gay Times)
ISBN 0 946745 75 7
Price £4.50 Pbk

Relative to Me...
Short stories on family life. Families can be a source of inspiration - or desperation! The stories in *Relative to Me...* show both, with a wonderful mix of serious and light-hearted writing.
'Relative to Me... proves there's plenty of talent just waiting to burst forth from the region.'
(Manchester Metro News)
'Twenty refreshingly original tales.' (The Teacher)
ISBN 0 946745 70 6
Price £3.95 Pbk

Talkers Through Dream Doors
Fourteen talented Black women write about their lives in this collection of poetry and short stories.
'These voices reassert the Black identity and cross new boundaries to redefine it.'
(Amrit Wilson)
ISBN 0 946745 60 9
Price £3.50 Pbk

Now Then
Poetry and short stories illustrating lifestyles, work and leisure from 1945 to the present day.
'An extremely poignant evocation of times and places that no longer exist.' (Eileen Derbyshire - Coronation Street's Emily Bishop)

ISBN 0 946745 55 2
Price £3.50 Pbk

Holding Out
Women's lives are portrayed with realism, frankness and fun in this excellent collection of twenty-one short stories.
ISBN 0 946745 30 7
Price £3.50 Pbk

Other titles from Commonword

Black and Priceless, poetry and short stories.
0 946745 45 5, £3.50
Between Mondays, poetry from the Monday Night Group. 0 946745 35 8, £2.50
Identity Magazine, poetry and articles by Asian and African-Caribbean writers. £0.95
Liberation Soldier, poetry by Joe Smythe.
0 946745 25 0, £2.50
Poetic Licence, poetry from Greater Manchester.
0 946745 40 4, £2.50
Turning Points, a Northern Gay Writers collection.
0 946745 20 X, £2.95

For a recent catalogue of all our titles, write to:
Crocus books/ Commonword
Cheetwood House
21 Newton Street
Manchester M1 1FZ.

If you are visually impaired and would like this book or any of our other titles to be produced on audio-tape please contact us.

ORDER FORM

TITLE	QUANTITY	PRICE	AMOUNT
Crocus Five Women Poets		£5.95	
Dancing on Diamonds		£5.95	
The Delicious Lie		£4.95	
Rainbows In The Ice		£4.50	
A Matter of Fat		£4.95	
Herzone		£4.50	
Flame		£4.50	
Beyond Paradise		£4.50	
Relative to Me...		£3.95	
Talkers Through Dream Doors		£3.50	
Now Then		£3.50	
Black and Priceless		£3.50	
Holding Out		£3.50	
Identity Magazine		£0.95	
Poetic Licence		£2.50	
Between Mondays		£2.50	
Liberation Soldier		£2.50	
Turning Points		£2.95	

TOTAL_____

Please send a cheque or postal order, made payable to Commonword Ltd, covering the purchase price plus 50p per book postage and packing.

NAME..

ADDRESS..

....

...............................POSTCODE..........................

Please return to: Commonword, Cheetwood House, 21 Newton Street, Manchester M1 1FZ.